Design	Cooper–West
Editor	Tessa Board
Art Director	Charles Matheson
Researcher	John MacClancy
Consultant	Joyce Pope
Illustrations	Cooper–West
	Rob Shone

Designed and produced by
Aladdin Books Ltd
70 Old Compton Street
London W1

Published in the USA in 1984 by
Franklin Watts
387 Park Avenue South
New York, NY 10016

Library of Congress
Catalog Card No 84-51225

ISBN 0-531-04833-0

Printed in Italy

FRANKLIN WATTS PICTURE ATLAS

Forests

Dougal Dixon

FRANKLIN WATTS
London · New York · Toronto · Sydney

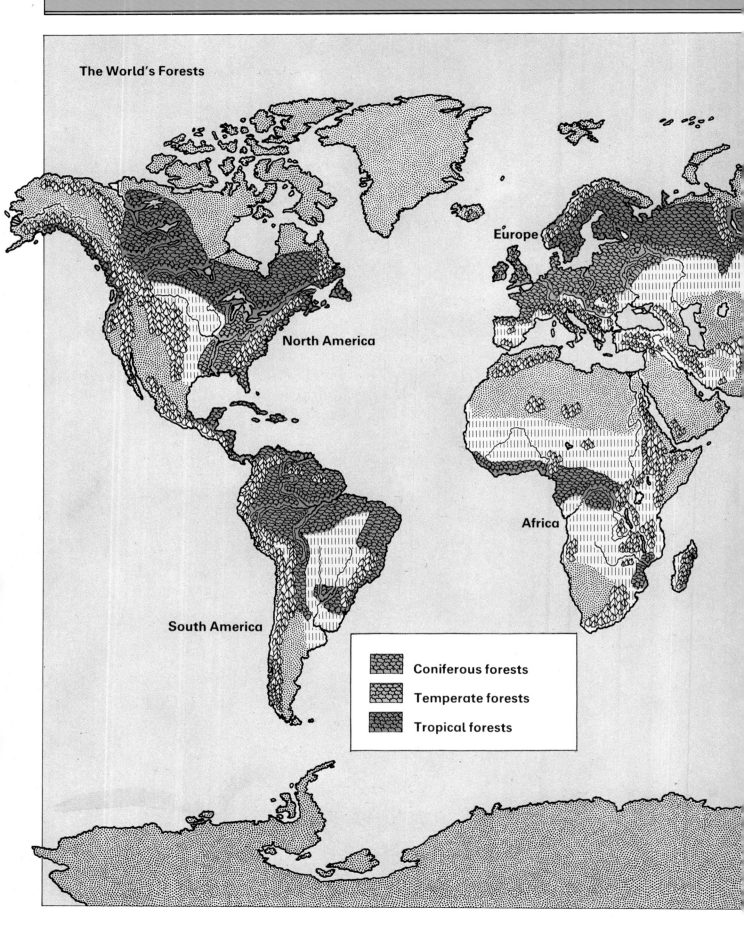

The World's Forests

Europe

North America

Africa

South America

Coniferous forests

Temperate forests

Tropical forests

Foreword

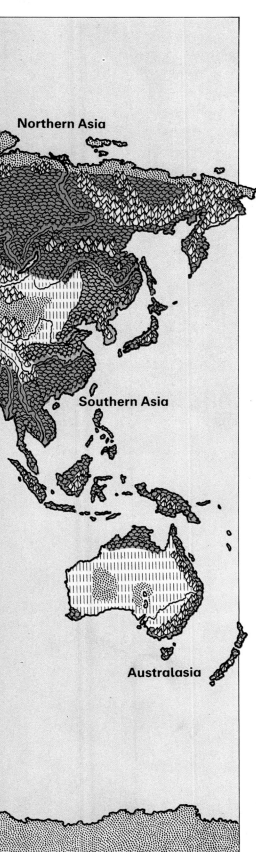

Northern Asia

Southern Asia

Australasia

Enter a forest and you enter another world, a world that closes in around you and cuts you off from the open country you left behind. In a forest there are no horizons; even the sky may be hidden from view by the lofty branches of tall trees. In stories and legends, woods and forests are places of mystery and magic, and even though we no longer believe in such things, forests still tend to be silent and secretive places, full of interest and beauty. They are some of the few remaining wild places where plants and animals can live undisturbed by humans.

In the past, there were people who lived in and off the forests, and a few still do today. But humans had little impact on forests until relatively recently, when demand for more food and land for an ever-increasing population resulted in forest clearance on a large scale. In addition, human activities are now affecting the world's few remaining forests. For example, the loss of huge tracts of Amazonian jungle is seriously affecting not only the ecological environment of the area, but also the amount of oxygen that they contribute to the atmosphere. This will eventually affect the world's climate.

Contents

Forest Types

The world's forests are of three different types: coniferous, temperate broadleaved and tropical forests. Coniferous forests spread across the northern parts of Europe, Asia and North America, and on mountain slopes further south where the climate is similar to that in the north.

The word coniferous means "cone-bearing" — all the coniferous trees reproduce from seeds that grow inside cones. Most conifers are evergreens; they lose and replace their leaves gradually throughout the year.

Temperate forests grow in mild, rainy climates. In these temperate climates broadleaved trees are deciduous. This means that they lose all their leaves in autumn, and the trees lie dormant during winter when water and nutrients (foods) are difficult to obtain from the soil.

Tropical forests grow where there is almost constant sunshine and the average temperature is about 25°C (77°F). Rainfall is usually over 1500 mm (59 in) a year. In some areas, rain may fall in all seasons or only in one or two. For example, in parts of India the rains come during the monsoons, which occur once or twice a year. Here the tropical forests are mainly deciduous. The trees lose their leaves before the drier season starts and so conserve water.

In tropical rain forests, such as those in South America, up to 2500 mm (98 in) of rain falls throughout the year, and the tallest trees grow to a height of 50 m (164 ft). The trees are mostly evergreens, with broad leaves that have a shiny surface to discourage lichens and mosses growing on them.

Comparative heights of the different forest types

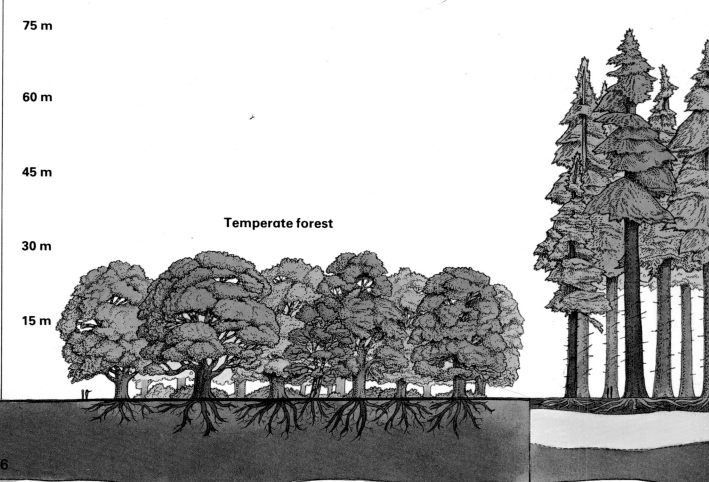

75 m

60 m

45 m

Temperate forest

30 m

15 m

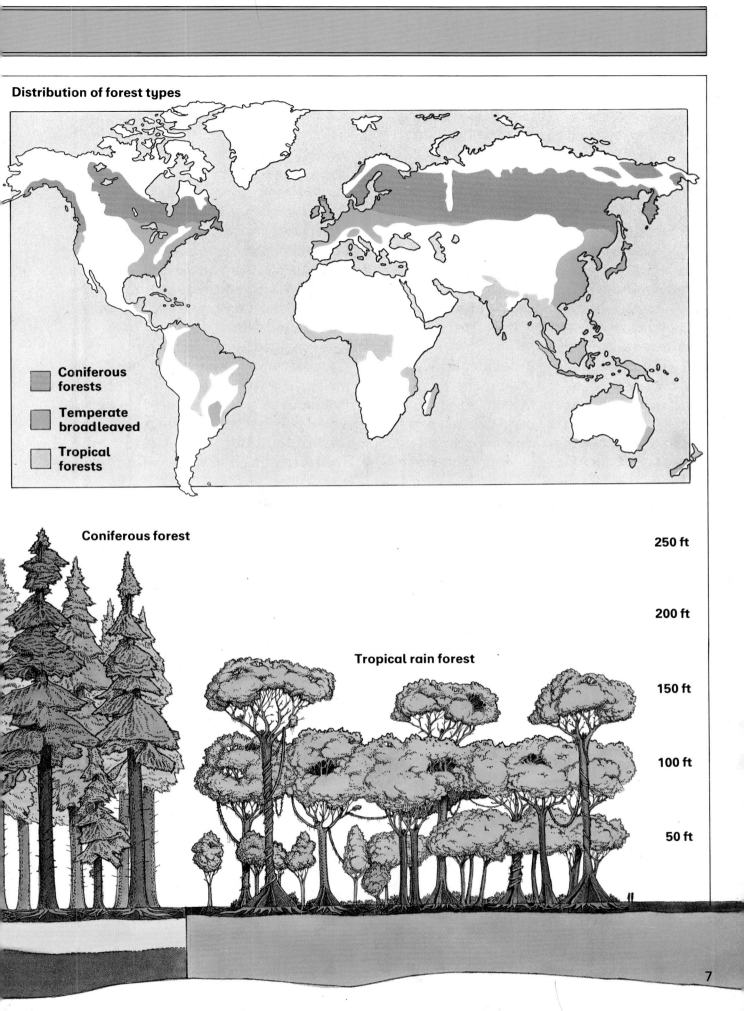

Distribution of forest types

Coniferous forests

Temperate broadleaved

Tropical forests

Coniferous forest

Tropical rain forest

250 ft

200 ft

150 ft

100 ft

50 ft

How the Forest Works

Because climate varies from one area of the world to another, the world can be divided into different climatic *zones*, or areas. In each zone the climate makes conditions right for certain types of plants to grow. Scientists describe these as zones of vegetation. Although a particular zone may have many different types of plants growing in it there is usually one type that is the naturally dominant, or main, type. Forests are one kind of vegetation zone. They occur in areas that have more than 250 mm (10 in) of rain a year and more than 30 days a year when the temperature is at least 10°C (50°F).

Trees are the dominant kind of plant in a forest, but in most cases other kinds of plants grow there too. All these plants, and the climate of the area, make up a special environment.

As with all living things, forests are dependent on water. The diagram below shows how water, through the processes of evaporation and rainfall, works in a continuous cycle.

The forest ecosystem

An ecosystem is the name for all the non-living substances and living organisms that make up such an environment.

Like all ecosystems, a forest has four basic parts which work together. First, there are the non-living things such as air and moisture (1), the Sun (2), and minerals such as phosphates and nitrates. These are necessary for the growth of plants. Second, there are living organisms that produce food. Most of these are green plants (3) which, by using the Sun's energy, are able to combine water with carbon dioxide from the air to produce foods. Living organisms that consume, or eat, the plants (4), and those that eat the plant-eaters (5), make up the third part. Finally, there are living things such as bacteria and fungi (6), that break down tissues of dead plants and animals (7, 8), into chemical materials. These chemicals are returned to the soil, to be taken up by plant roots and used again for growth.

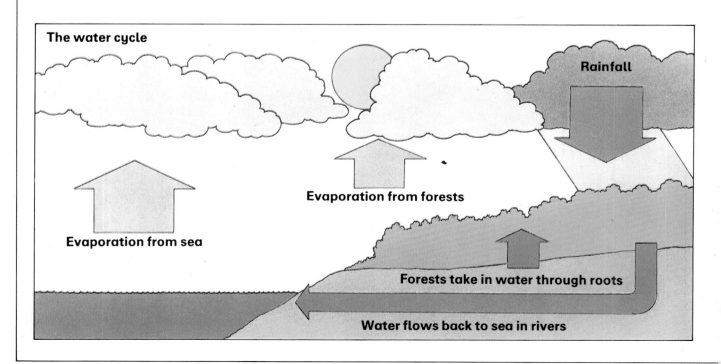

The water cycle

Rainfall

Evaporation from forests

Evaporation from sea

Forests take in water through roots

Water flows back to sea in rivers

Forest ecosystem

Timber wolf

Canadian lumberjack

Pulp mill

Grizzly bear

Charcoal production

Giant redwood

Florida Indians

Mexican plantation

In prehistoric times great belts of forests stretched across North America, Europe and Asia. The remnants of these forests still exist as an 800 km (500-mile) wide belt reaching from the United States northern border as far north as trees can grow, and also along the mountainous west coast south in to the United States. This is coniferous forest. In California it is home to both the biggest trees in the world – the giant redwoods – and the oldest – the bristlecone pines. In the Rocky Mountains some of the bristlecones are over 4500 years old.

Broadleaved forests of oaks, maples, hickories and chestnuts once stretched from the east coast of North America to the Mississippi River. This was the first area colonized by Europeans 400 years ago. They found the soil so fertile that the forests were cleared bit by bit for farms, or for growing tobacco and cotton. However, one large forest remains in the Appalachian Mountains.

Farther south in the tropical forests of Mexico, large areas have been similarly cleared in order to grow commercial fruit crops. In the southeast of the United States, semitropical conditions and floods have resulted in forests of deciduous conifers – the swamp cypresses.

Coniferous forests

Temperate forests

Tropical forests

Maple trees, Canada

Until the arrival of the Europeans, the native peoples of the North American forests lived by hunting and gathering. They hunted with bow and arrow, or set traps for their prey, which included bear, moose, deer and wolf. People that lived near rivers or the coast were also capable fishermen. On the northwest coast, tribes such as the Haida, Nootka and Kwakiutl built permanent villages of wooden houses, and were famous for their arts, particularly their carved totem poles. In the southeast, Indian tribes living in the Everglade swamps had a lifestyle not unlike that of the river tribes living in Amazonia today.

However, whites have been using the forests for centuries. First they trapped animals for furs but now one of the more important industries is logging. Once the logs are cut, they are moved by floating them down rivers to saw mills or factories, where they are processed into paper, cellulose or charcoal.

Floating logs downriver, Canada

Coniferous habitation

Looking at the vast North American continent from the top downward, the first forest type we meet is the great coniferous forest of Canada and certain parts of the United States. Here the trees can grow only in the long days of summer. Squirrels, mice and crossbills feed on the pine seeds, deer such as wapiti and moose browse on the vegetation and birds and carnivorous mammals such as the wolf and grizzly bear find plenty to hunt. However, summer lasts only three months, and in the cold, dark days of

Giant redwood tree, California

winter nothing grows. Some animals hibernate, others move south, leaving the forest empty and silent. The many species of pine trees growing in these boreal forests seldom grow higher than 30 m (100 ft). Their tall straight trunks, easily stripped of their branches, are ideal for the lumber industry. Pine wood is called "softwood" since it is more easily worked and not as durable as the wood of many broadleaved trees. Farther south, the giant redwoods are also softwoods. Their vast size is partially due to the fertile soil of the west coast, where they grow in river valleys.

Mixed forests
The humid conditions in the northwestern United States produce a lush mixed forest of maple, Douglas fir, red cedar and Sitka spruce. By contrast, the hot, dry summers of the southwest result in drought conditions that are more suitable to conifers, such as cypresses and junipers, whose leaves are resistant to water loss.

Everglades
The best known swamp forest is the Florida Everglades. It is a flooded basin in which islands of trees can be seen, the roots mostly underwater. Special air-breathing growths rise vertically from the roots of swamp cypresses to take in oxygen from the air, an adaptation which is also found in the trees of the mangroves that fringe the Everglades. Herons and cormorants are among the birds that fish in the swamps, and the whole area abounds in reptiles and amphibians, including alligators and snakes.

Wolf

Bull moose

Hummingbird

Anaconda

Balsa raft

Amazonian tribesman

Sloth

Coffee production

Evergreen oak

South America

The greatest area of forest in South America lies in the basin of the Amazon and Orinoco Rivers. It is the largest continuous tropical rain forest in the world, each hectare (2.5 acres) of which has been estimated to support 25 tonnes (25.4 tons) of living material. Much of this biological wealth is in the canopy, the topmost forest layer, where large trees and creepers form their branches and leaves. Here, too, most plants produce their flowers and fruits, including orchids, bromeliads and other "epiphytes" that anchor themselves, like the climbers, to other plants. This forest has more epiphytes and creepers than any other.

Tropical and mixed forests also grow along the Andes Mountains and in southern Brazil. In places on the mountain slopes they form "cloud" forests, so called because the canopy is shrouded in mist. This increased dampness encourages not only epiphytes on the trees, but also ferns and mosses.

In Chile and Argentina, the striking monkey puzzle tree, up to 30 m (100 ft) tall, looms out of the mists. It is a pine, and grows in mixed temperate forests with Patagonian cedars. Elsewhere southern beeches are dominant, some kinds being deciduous, others evergreen.

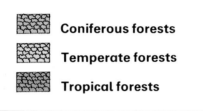

Coniferous forests

Temperate forests

Tropical forests

The Amazonian rain forest from the air

Wildlife

Compared with the rain forests of Africa and Asia, there are fewer large land animals in South and Central America. The largest plant-eaters are tapirs, small deer, and the semiaquatic capybara, all of which are hunted by the jaguar. Other large predators are the caimans, relatives of the alligator, and the world's largest snake, the anaconda.

But while the forest floor is sparsely populated, the canopy is alive with animal life, particularly birds. More than half the world's bird species live in tropical South America. Tiny, jewel-colored hummingbirds sip nectar from flowers; gaudily-marked toucans collect fruit with their huge beaks; and noisy macaws extract Brazil nuts from their husks. Many of the monkeys, as well as other kinds of mammals, such as tree anteaters, tree porcupines, and kinkajous, live in the canopy. The sloth spends its whole life in the canopy and rarely comes down to ground level.

Trees and trade

Far less of the Amazon has been exploited for its lumber than in Southeast Asia or Africa. An exception is the true mahogany, a strong and straight-grained hardwood, which is now quite rare. Hardwood refers to the usually denser wood of broadleaved trees, but American balsa is an exceptionally light hardwood and is grown commercially in Ecuador. Commercial products of the forest include greenheart timber, which decays very slowly in water, and is used for piles in harbors, and the basralocus wood which is used for shipbuilding. Coffee is grown extensively on plantations carved from the original forest.

Giant sloth

In the interior

Anaconda

The livelihood of the native tribes, the Yanommi for example, depends on their knowledge of the forest. To catch fish and hunt wild animals, and gather fruits, nuts, honey and roots for food they must know the growing cycles of forest trees and the behavior of the animals. The forest provides them with fibers for spinning cloth, and weaving baskets, poles for the making of shelters and leaves for thatching. Fuel is always available, and they know how to use concoctions from plants to treat ailments.

Such small tribes were once scattered throughout the Amazon and had little effect on it. Where they cultivated the land, it was on such a small scale that the forest soon grew back over exhausted plots. An attempt has been made to keep 12 of the tribes free from the influences of modern civilization. But the building of the Trans-Amazonian highway shattered the dream. The highway has opened up new areas for logging and mining, but far more forest has been destroyed by the road-building itself.

New farming communities are different from the old hunting tribes in their effect on the forest. Some are Indian tribes who have gradually settled down after a nomadic life, while others are new farmers who have left the towns. Both practice "slash-and-burn" techniques, cutting and burning sections of forest in order to cultivate it. This destroys the thin leaf-litter containing the essential nutrients on the forest floor. The high competition for land has resulted in clearings being reused after too short a break, before the soil has had a chance to recover from supporting previous harvests. Crops fail, and the soil becomes completely eroded.

Yanommi women

Slash-and-burn cultivation in the Amazon jungle

Swedish logger

Wooden houses

Paper mill

Pine plantation

Dutch elm beetle

Backpacking

European fox

Cutting cork

Olive groves

Europe

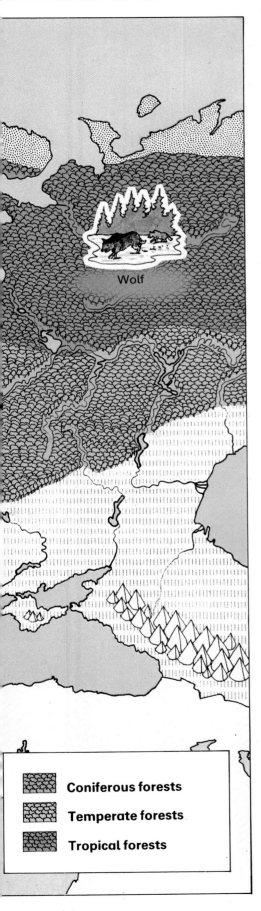

Wolf

Coniferous forests

Temperate forests

Tropical forests

Vast forests once covered a great deal of Europe, the same as the boreal forests did in North America and northern Asia. There are still remnants of coniferous forests in the mountainous areas like the Alps, the Pyrenees and the Carpathians. In other places the natural vegetation is a mixture of oaks, beeches, sycamores and birches. But since the soil on which these broadleaved trees grow is deep, fertile and particularly suited to agriculture, most of the great forests of the past have long since disappeared.

Where the soil is sufficiently deep, the oak, of which there are hundreds of different types, is the dominant species of the European woodland scene. Tall beeches grow, sometimes as natural "monocultures," on chalky soil. Ashes too favor chalky soil, and tend to grow in open woodland. On the northern fringes of the temperate woods, where the soil is poorer, willows and birches mingle with coniferous trees to form mixed forests.

In the Mediterranean region, where summers are hot and dry and winters mild and wet, evergreen broadleafs and conifers grow together. Both have thick tough leaves which conserve water. Evergreen cork oaks, which grow in countries around the Mediterranean, have bark 30 cm (1 ft) or more thick, which is commercially harvested from growing trees. Another familiar Mediterranean broadleaved tree is the olive, which has been cultivated for its fruit for well over 2000 years.

Deciduous forest in summer, W. Germany.

Many of the remaining forests and woodlands in Europe have survived because they were once part of the huge estates of the nobility. From the Middle Ages on, these estates were the home of deer, boar, foxes, badgers and otters where they were hunted for sport and food. Now many of these forests are used for recreation and kept especially for animals to breed. This kind of wildlife management is an effective form of conservation for animals and trees alike. In France, for example, whole areas of forest are banned to humans, allowing no interference to the natural environment.

In former times predatory animals such as bears, lynx and wolves roamed free through the forests. Nowadays these predators are found only in remote, sparsely populated mountainous areas because they have been hunted to protect crops and domestic livestock. The absence of these predators, however, has allowed other forest animals such as squirrels, stoats, woodpeckers, warblers and deer to survive in abundance.

Two distinctive features of the temperate deciduous forests are the shrub and herb layers. Trees often flower in spring before their leaves unfurl, and are pollinated by the wind. The ground, therefore, is open to the sunlight and carpets of flowering herbs and shrubs grow on the floor of the forest. During the summer fruits ripen, to be eaten and then dispersed by the animals. Most animals find food and shelter throughout the winter, although some hibernate.

As well as being cleared for agriculture, Europe's temperate deciduous forests have been ravaged for ship-building, by wars, and for charcoal burning. Until the Industrial Revolution of the late 18th century, when coal and coke began to replace charcoal as industrial fuel, huge areas of forests were destroyed. Charcoal

Results of Dutch elm disease

Red squirrels

is still used as a filter in certain industrial processes, and as fuel in countries without coal, oil or gas.

Dying trees

Not all the changes to Europe's forests have been caused directly by man. In the 1970s, Dutch elm disease attacked and killed millions of elm trees. In England and Wales 20 million trees died, two-thirds of the British elm population. Caused by fungal infection, the disease is spread by the elm bark beetle. Another threat to European trees is definitely man-made. Called "acid rain," it is caused by sulphur dioxide produced as waste from coal- and oil-burning industries. Sulphur combines with water in the atmosphere to fall as acidic rain over the trees. Two million hectares (4.9 million acres) of central Europe's forests are dying, including 40 per cent of pine and spruce trees in West Germany's Black Forest.

As on every other continent, in Europe certain forests have become recreational parks and wildlife reserves. Today's city dwellers, vacationing and "getting back to nature," put on backpacks and go trekking and camping to enjoy the outdoors and the wildlife of the forest. But other parts of Europe, Scandinavia especially, depend on the forests for industry and building – Scandinavian countries are famous for their wooden buildings. Finland is the most densely forested country in Europe. It is a major producer of cut timber, paper, plywood and cellulose.

In certain countries like Germany and Scotland reafforestation is being carried out. This is the replanting of trees where agriculture or industry has previously stripped them away.

Badger

Backpacking in the Black Forest, W. Germany

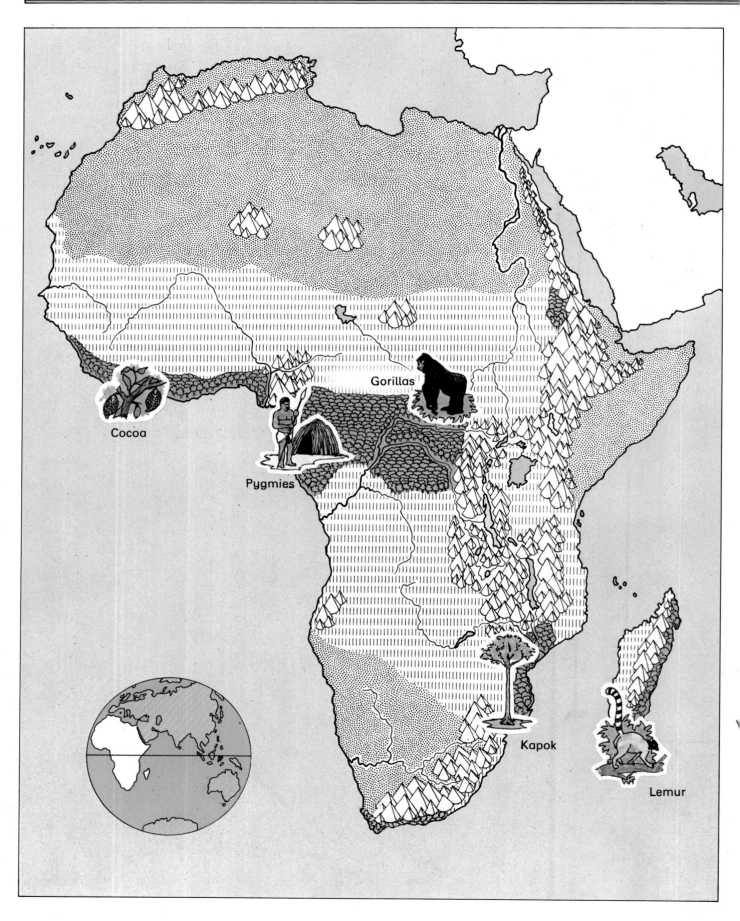

Cocoa

Pygmies

Gorillas

Kapok

Lemur

Though Africa contains less forest than other tropical countries, there is a mass of tropical rain forest in western and central equatorial Africa, forming an almost continuous canopy, except for patches of savannah. The main trees forming the canopy can go up to 40 m (134 ft), while even taller trees, called emergents, tower as high as 60 m (197 ft). These include the African kapok and red ironwood tree.

At its center, this forest consists mainly of evergreen deciduous trees, but toward its edges, and in West Africa, the proportion of only deciduous trees gradually grows.

Another change in the look of the forest occurs from lowland to mountain regions. In the lowlands there are many giant trees, with buttressed trunks. In the mountains trees do not grow quite as tall and buttresses are rare. There are also fewer climbers, but a greater number of epiphytes such as mosses, lichens, orchids and ferns growing on the trees in mountain regions. In parts of east Africa, the highest mountain forests contain strange giant "flowers" — such as groundsels and lobelias — that grow nowhere else on Earth. Tropical rain forests also grow along the wet east coast of Madagascar.

Coniferous forests

Temperate forests

Tropical forests

Jungle skyline, West Africa

To most people, the monkeys and apes are the most familiar animals of the tropical rain forest, and in Africa there are two groups of forest apes, the gorillas and the chimpanzees. Gorillas are true forest animals, although the big males are too heavy to climb far up into the trees. Other members of the family, however, feed and rest in the lower branches and may make their nests in small trees. The smaller chimpanzees can travel equally well in the trees or on the ground. Like gorillas, they make a nest every evening out of leaves and branches.

Monkeys of different kinds make use of all levels of the forest from the ground to the canopy. This means that even if their territories overlap, two different species do not compete with each other for food. The almost tailless drill and mandrill feed on fallen fruit on the ground; mangabeys live mostly in the lower branches of the trees; while the strikingly-patterned guenons feed at different levels of the leafy canopy, mainly eating fruit. Another group of monkeys, the colobi, are exclusively leaf-eaters, and have a complex stomach to help in the digestion of their tough food.

In Madagascar's forests there is a different group of monkey-like animals, called lemurs. The largest lemur, the indri, has practically no tail, but others, including the white sifaka and the ring-tailed lemurs, use their long tails as balancers when they climb and jump in the branches. Ring-tailed lemurs also use their distinctive tails as a warning signal as they move about in a group.

Jungle flight

Tropical forest birds feed on fruit, insects, or a mixture of both. In Africa, the Guinea fowl and bareheaded rock fowl are both inconspicuous ground-dwellers. But in the canopy live many small, colorful birds,

Buttress roots on the forest floor

insectivorous flycatchers and warblers, and the fruit-eating pigeons and parrots.

Fruit-eating bats are flying mammals that spend the day roosting in tall trees. At night they flock to feed on fig or other fruit trees. The scaly-tailed flying squirrels cannot really fly, but can glide from one tree to another to seek out edible fruits.

Gorilla

White sifakas

One of the native groups of the African tropical forest are the Pygmies, a small race of people averaging 1.4 m (4.5 ft) in height. They look on the forest as their kindly food provider, and as a force to be respected and trusted. In fact they call the forest "mother" or "father" in their language. The Bantu peoples just outside of the forest are afraid of it, and this fear has helped the Pygmies protect their homes and prevent them from being overrun. The Pygmies willingly trade such things as meat, ivory, nuts and other products of the forest with the Bantu, as well as performing tasks for them such as thatching, and helping with their harvests. In return the Pygmies receive clothing, tools, beans, bananas and salt. The Bantu look on the Pygmies as slaves, but the Pygmies find the relationship to their advantage, because their villages – and the forest – are left alone.

Commercial products from the African tropical forests include the cola nut, coffee, cocoa and oil palm. The latter has a wide variety of uses ranging from cooking oil to engine fuel.

Pygmy with an elephant spear

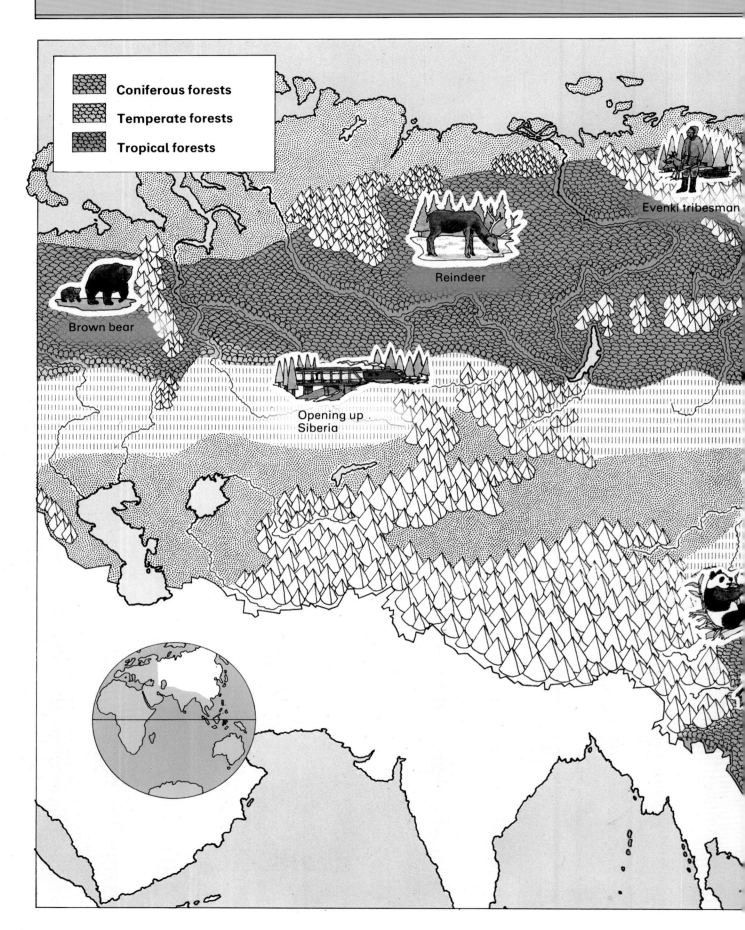

Coniferous forests

Temperate forests

Tropical forests

Brown bear

Reindeer

Evenki tribesman

Opening up
Siberia

Northern Asia

Bamboo
forest

Across northern Asia stretches a vast sea of conifers – the great Siberian forest, covering an area a third larger than the United States. In the west, spruce, pine and fir are the dominant species. The Yenisei river forms a natural divide, for the drier conditions to the east of the river favor the growth of larches. Larches are deciduous conifers. They drop their needles in autumn and stand bare-branched when the soil is frozen in winter.

The band of forest that borders the Pacific Ocean alters dramatically in appearance from the north to the south. At its northernmost limit, where winters are longest, the trees are small and scattered as in a parkland. Then the great forests of Siberian and Dahurian larch, which grow to about 30 m (100 ft), take over in cooler mountainous areas. But as the climate becomes more temperate, with longer, wetter summers, broadleaved trees mix with conifers.

Further south still, in the warm temperate forests of China, there are so many different species of broadleaves growing together that the forests look like tropical rain forests. Bamboos often grow here, and some species of these enormous grasses can reach 30 m (100 ft). Others form dense impenetrable forests, as in western China where the giant panda lives.

Taiga, Siberia

Southern Asia and Australasia

Rain falls all through the year in Malaya, Sumatra and Borneo, where a huge variety of species flourish in the tropical rain forests. In Malaya there are 2500 species of tall trees alone. The coconut-bearing palm tree grows extensively throughout this region.

Elsewhere in southern Asia, the heaviest rainfall comes during one season of the year. The tropical forests contain many deciduous trees that drop their leaves before the drier part of the year, and grow new ones in time for the rains. One such family of trees is the dipterocarps, a name which means that their fruits have two wings to help in seed dispersal. Borneo alone has 270 species of dipterocarps. Some grow to 70 m (230 ft) and are supported at the base of their trunks by huge buttresses.

Nowhere in Southeast Asia is very far from water, and when river meets sea, there may be forests of mangroves. The trees of the mangrove swamps cope with the problem of mud and salt water by devices such as stilt roots, leaves that excrete salt, and air-breathing root extensions.

Throughout all of Australia's forests, whether they are tropical, temperate or dry, the majority of the tree species are aromatic eucalypts or gums. A few conifers grow in Southeast Asia and Australasia, in particular the kauri pine, which reaches to northern New Zealand.

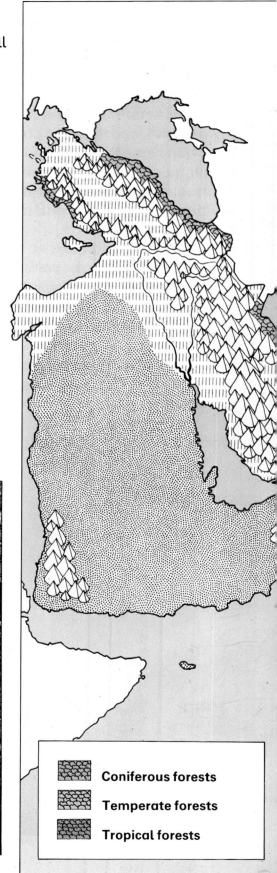

Coniferous forests

Temperate forests

Tropical forests

Monsoon forest

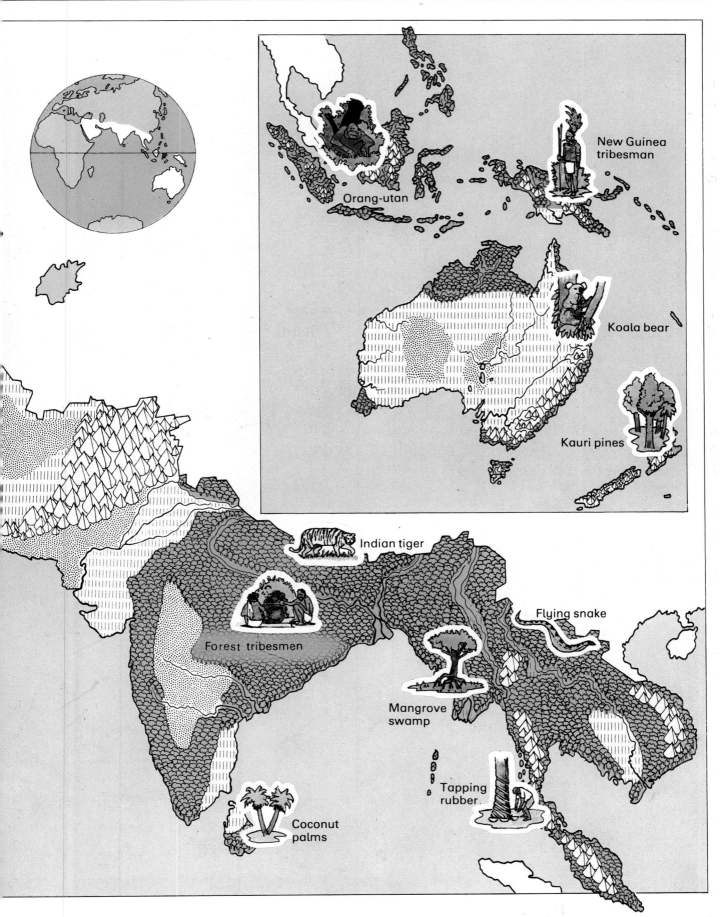

Orang-utan

New Guinea tribesman

Koala bear

Kauri pines

Indian tiger

Flying snake

Forest tribesmen

Mangrove swamp

Tapping rubber

Coconut palms

More types of mammals live on the forest floor in the tropical forests of southern Asia than in Africa or South America. There are small buffalo, deer and antelope, wild pigs and tapirs – and preying on them are the leopard and the tiger. Only adult rhinoceroses and elephants are safe from the tiger. This big cat seeks out thick, shady parts of the forest, and lies in wait for its prey.

Among the tree-dwelling animals of the Asian tropical forest are many gliders, which use extensions of their skin to spread their weight and catch air currents as they jump from tree to tree. Flying squirrels and colugos are mammals, but there are also "flying" frogs, lizards and snakes. Pythons also lurk in the lower branches of trees.

The gibbons and the orang-utans use a different method of travel, but one that is also very suitable for a forest existence. Tucking their back legs out of the way, they swing hand over hand from branch to branch. The lightweight gibbons are particularly adept at this movement and can gain enough momentum to swing across a 15 m (50 ft) gap.

Australasia

The rain forests of New Guinea contain a mixture of southern Asian and Australian animals, but, surprisingly, there are no large carnivores. The biggest meat-eaters are lizards, pythons and boas, and a cat-like marsupial. This situation is of benefit to small forest mammals and birds, and as a result there are more birds of paradise in New Guinea than in Australia. The male birds of paradise

Koala bear in a eucalyptus tree, Australia

have elaborate plumage and perform extraordinary displays to their dull-looking females.

Some marsupials live on New Guinea, but Australia is their main stronghold. Many live in the eucalyptus forests, including the koala. The koala is one of the most arboreal (tree-living) of all animals, only coming down to the ground in order to get to another gum tree. It has a diet that is exclusively eucalyptus, preferring the tips of the youngest leaves.

Most kangaroos and wallabies live on the ground, but there are a few tree-dwelling species. Their front legs are nearly as long as their back legs, and they have strong claws to pull themselves up the trees. Tree kangaroos are quite nimble and can jump easily downwards from branch to branch.

There are places on the many scattered, highly-forested islands of Southeast Asia where tribes have remained living in the Stone Age. The Tasaday of Mindanao still use stone tools and collect such things as nuts, grubs, frogs and small fish from streams. They have no weapons, in fact they have no word in their language for war. The Punan of Sarawak, on the other hand, are mainly hunters. They are very good shots and can kill a gibbon 50 m (164 ft) away with a blowpipe. The forested mountains of New Guinea are also home to many various tribes who are famous for their elaborate ceremonial costumes.

In parts of northern India, the home of the Naga tribe, the slopes of the Himalayas have been cleared of forest. Along with Burma, this is one of the world's biggest producers of tea. On the island of Sumatra and in Malaya, rubber is harvested extensively.

Bird of paradise, New Guinea

Python

New Guinea tribesman

The Future of the Environment

The forests are vulnerable. Since the coming of man the forests in the temperate regions have been gradually cleared away. Industrialized Europe has been stripped of its great trees – Great Britain having lost 95 per cent of its original forest; France, Spain, Belgium, Italy and Greece, 80 to 90 per cent; and Sweden and Finland, 50 per cent. The United States has lost 50 per cent of its forest in 300 years of continual exploitation.

Civilized man has an insatiable need for wood and its products. A typical house in Europe or North America uses 43 m^3 (56 yd^3) of timber. Paper is one of the most important of the wood products. In the industrialized countries each person uses about 300 kg (660 lb) of paper every year.

Although forests have been of economic benefit to humans throughout the ages, they are also essential in maintaining the proper level of oxygen in the atmosphere for us to breathe. Industry produces a great deal of poisonous carbon dioxide, and the world's forest areas are needed to convert this back into oxygen. The few hundred trees of the Bois de Boulogne in Paris are barely enough to replace the oxygen in the air used up by the airplanes at Orly airport. As the oxygen balance in the air changes, so slowly does the climate, therefore, changing the ecology.

Much modern industry still relies on "non-renewable" fossil fuels. These are coal and lignite from forests, and oil from

Road construction in Amazonia

sea creatures, and were made many millions of years ago and stored in the rocks. Once they are used up there will be no more. Forests, on the other hand, can and do grow continually in areas re-planted specifically for this reason. Wood can be harvested as fuel and more can be grown. It is cheaper to use the fossil fuels, but scientists are developing chemical processes to turn wood into an alcohol that can be used to fuel cars and other machines.

The big problem is proper manage-ment – keeping enough areas planted with young trees to supply needs in decades to come, and choosing the right species. Cleared areas of tropical forest expose the weak jungle soil to the weather and wash it away, forming deserts that cannot be turned back into forests. Any cleared area here reduces the amount of water that is returned to the atmosphere by evaporation from the leaves. Hence, less rain falls on other areas of the forest. In temperate regions it is tempting to plant forests with a single fast-growing species, such as spruce. But these single species "monoculture" woodlands are not so attractive to wildlife and as a result, are not so attractive for recreational purposes.

As time goes on the forests will become more and more valuable. It is going to be very important to look after the forests that remain so that they will still be here to benefit the generations to come.

The disappearing jungle – a modern settlement

Interesting Facts

Some species of bamboo have growth rates of 90 cm (3 ft) per day, they can reach a height of 30 m (100 ft) in three months.

Rafflesia, found in the jungles of Southeast Asia, has the largest of all flowers, which can grow up to 90 cm (3 ft) across.

2000 sq km (772 sq miles) of tropical rain forest have been lost in the Amazon basin by roadbuilding, simply to enable people to get into the area!

The wooded area of the USSR is 1093 million hectares (2700 million acres), an area about the size of Australia, and amounting to 25 per cent of the world's forests.

The world's tallest tree is a Giant Redwood, found in California. It stands up to 112 m (367 ft) tall — over twice the size of Nelson's column in London.

Hummingbirds can fly forward at about 40-50 km (25-30 miles) per hour. The humming sound they make, that gives them their name, is caused by the rapid beating of their wings.

The oldest in the world is a bristlecone pine located in Nevada. It was found to be about 4500 years old.

The heaviest wood in the world is the black ironwood. It has a specific gravity of 1.49, almost 1.5 times as heavy as water.

The Banyan tree in Sri Lanka has more than 350 large "trunks" and over 3000 small ones.

The three-toed sloth of tropical America is the slowest-moving land mammal. Its usual ground speed is 2 m (7 ft) a minute.

The largest leaves of any plant are those of the African Raffia palm, which can be up to 12.2 m (40 ft) long.

The wood of the balsa tree is one of the lightest in the world. In 1947, the explorer Thor Heyerdahl sailed a raft of 9 balsa wood logs across the Pacific Ocean to prove that the South American Indians could have made the journey to the South Sea Islands, Easter Island in particular, many centuries ago.

The hardest of all woods comes from lignum vitae, an evergreen tree growing in tropical America. It used to be used for police truncheons!

If all the timber growing in the world today were suitable for building, it could provide three medium-sized houses for each person in the world.

Bristlecone pine

Location		Patient	Time		Received
From	To	Assignment	Departure	Arrival	By

Lutheran General Hospital
✚ Advocate

Patient Services
Patient Transportation Tally Sheet

Carts _____
W/C_____
Other_____
Cancelled _____

Name _____

Date _____

Location		Patient	Time		Received
From	To	Assignment	Departure	Arrival	By

Glossary

Scientists use many special words to describe forests and the wildlife found in forests. These are some of the common ones you are likely to come across.

Amphibians Animals that live both on land and in the water.

Arboreal Of, or relating to trees. An arboreal mammal, for example, lives in trees.

Aromatic A term meaning sweet-smelling.

Bacterium (plural Bacteria) A microscopic single-celled creature related to the fungi.

Boreal Northerly. Usually applied to the coniferous, forests near the Arctic Circle.

Broadleaf A tree, such as oak and maple, that has broad leaves rather than needles.

Bromeliad A kind of epiphytic herbaceous plant such as the pineapple.

Canopy The thick roof of branches and leaves in a forest.

Carnivores Flesh-eating animals.

Cloud Forest A forest in the tropics where the tops of the trees are constantly hidden in mists and clouds.

Conifer A tree, such as pine, that bears its seeds in cones. It has needles rather than broad leaves.

Deciduous A tree that loses its leaves at a particular time of the year.

Dipterocarp A family of trees, the fruit of which has two wings which help with seed dispersal.

Ecology A science which deals with the relation of living organisms to their surroundings, their habits, and ways of life.

Ecosystem A system of ecology used more specifically for a definite area or forest.

Emergent A tall tree of the tropical rain forest that towers over the canopy.

Epiphyte A plant that grows upon another, using it for support, not as a food source.

Evaporation A process of turning water into vapour and being absorbed into the air.

Fossil Fuels Fuels that were formed many millions of years ago and that have been stored deep in the rocks of the Earth.

Hibernate Animals, to escape the cold winter months, sleep to conserve body temperature and energy, when there is little food to be found on the snow-covered ground.

Marsupial A mammal which is distinguished from others by carrying its young in a special pouch on its stomach.

Monoculture The raising of a single species of tree.

Monsoon The rainy season that accompanies the wind in Southeast Asia. The wind blows from the southwest in the summer and from the northeast in the winter.

Nectar A sweet fluid produced by plants, used by bees to make honey.

Nomads People that are constantly moving from place to place.

Nutrient A substance that can be used as a food, or that can be made into a food.

Oxygen A colorless invisible gas that is the most important element of the air that we breathe.

Pollination The action of seed dispersal.

Predator An animal that hunts another animal.

Protein A complex chemical containing nitrogen, carbon, hydrogen and oxygen that is an important part of all living organisms like animal and plant bodies, and is essential to the diet of animals.

Swamp An area of wet, low-lying ground.

Tropics The area of the Earth that lies between the latitudes 23½°N and 23½°S. The sun passes directly overhead at all places in the tropics twice during the year.

Index